Sam the Sea Cow

Sam the Sea Cow

Francine Jacobs

Illustrations by Laura Kelly

Walker and Company  New York

This edition published in the United States of America in 1991
by Walker Publishing Company, Inc.

Published simultaneously in Canada by Thomas Allen & Son
Canada, Limited, Markham, Ontario

Library of Congress Cataloging-in-Publication Data

Jacobs, Francine.
[Sewer Sam, the Sea Cow]
Sam the Sea Cow / Francine Jacobs; illustrations by Laura Kelly.
p.   cm.
Originally published: Sewer Sam, the Sea Cow. New York: Walker, 1979.
Summary: Follows the adventures of a manatee, or sea cow, from
birth till after he leaves his mother.
ISBN 0-8027-8147-0 (rein). —ISBN 0-8027-7373-7 (pbk)
1. Manatees—Juvenile literature. [1. Manatees.] I. Kelly,
Laura, ill. II. Title.
QL737. S63J32 1992
599.5'5—dc20   91-30384
                                                 CIP
                                                 AC

Book Design by Georg Brewer

Printed in Hong Kong

2   4   6   8   10   9   7   5   3   1

For Elizabeth Rose, with much love

—F. J.

For my parents, Tom and Pat Harris, who've done more for me
than I can ever thank them for.

—L. K.

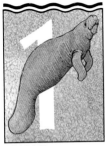

CHAPTER

Spring comes to southern Florida.
A huge, gray animal moves slowly
down a river toward the sea.
It is a shy, harmless manatee.

On her broad back, the manatee carries
a brand-new calf, just born.
He is three feet long
and weighs forty pounds.
His name will be Sam.

The manatee rises so her calf's head
is above the water.
Shoo-of! The calf breathes in.

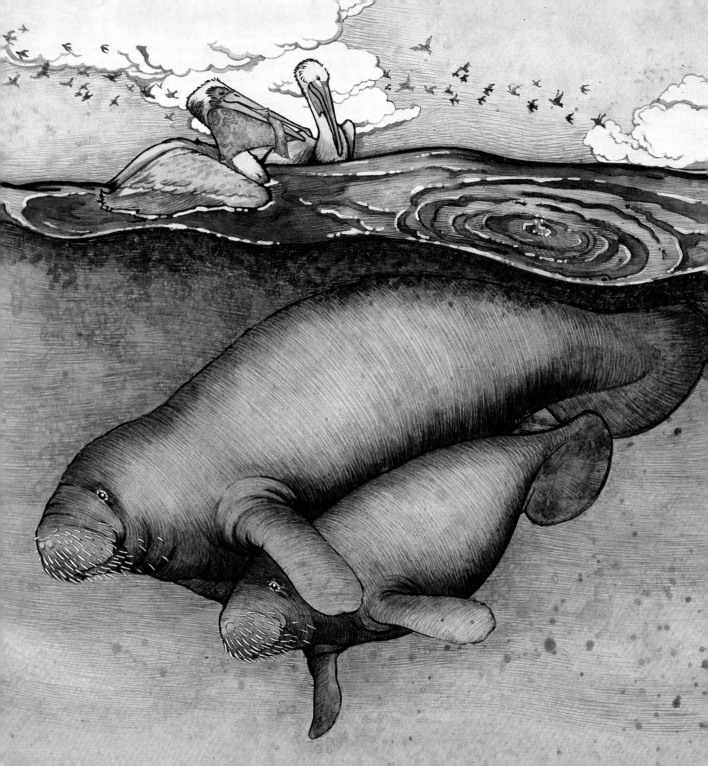

Aah-shoo! He breathes out.
Even though a manatee lives in the water,
it breathes air just like you and me.

Minutes go by.
Sam stays on his mother's back.
She ducks him.
Blub! Blub! Blub!
He bubbles.
Sam must hold his breath.
His mother lifts him into the air again.
Shoof-of! He snorts, happy for a breath.
His mother ducks him once more.
They practice this way until Sam
breathes in the air and
holds his breath underwater.

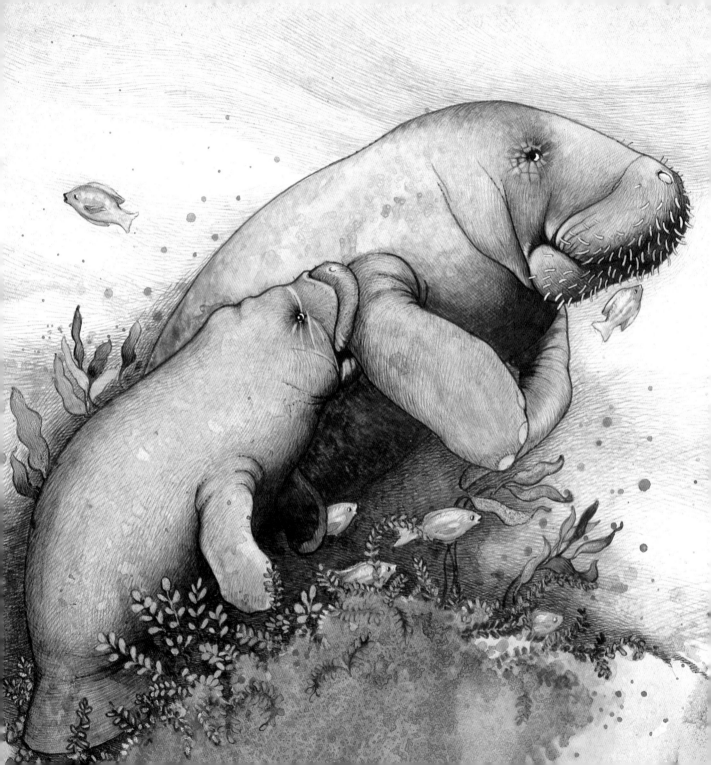

Manatees nurse their young in the water.

Sam finds a place beneath his mother's flipper
when he is hungry.

He sucks her warm milk.

Manatees are mammals like whales and dolphins.

Mammals feed their babies milk from special parts
of their bodies called mammary glands.

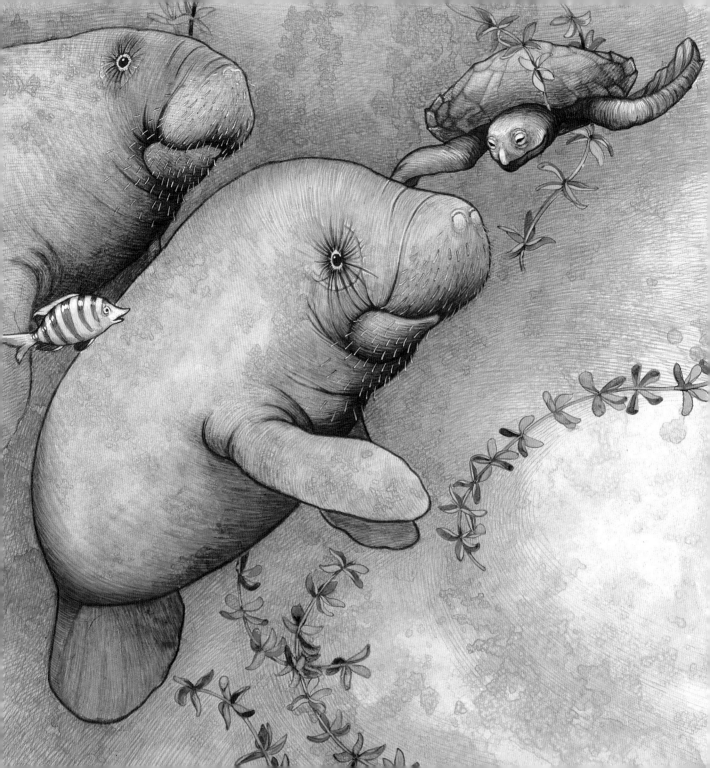

Sam follows his mother.

She swims with her big tail.

It is round and flat like a paddle.

Up and down it goes.

Sam swims with his two flippers.

They are shaped like mittens.

He will learn to use his tail later.

Sam looks like his mother.

He has little, round eyes and a small head.

He hears sounds

but he has no outside ears.

Sam's body is almost hairless.

It is shaped like a big pear.

Sam stays near his mother for months.

But one day Sam hears a strange noise.

Gr-r-r-r-r-r-r-r-r-r.

Sam is curious.

He lifts his head to look.

But he can't see far, not more than a foot.

Eep! Eep! Eep! His mother squeals to warn him.

BAM!!

Too late! A motorboat hits Sam. The propeller cuts him.

Sam tumbles over and over.

Surely he will drown . . . but

his mother catches him just in time.

She lifts him up to breathe.

Motorboats are manatees' worst enemies.

Luckily, Sam's skin is thick and tough.

His wound heals but leaves a scar between his eyes.

It will be there for the rest of his life.

Sam and his mother swim out to the sea.

Months go by.

It is fall.

They move back up a river to warmer waters.

Mangrove trees grow thickly along the banks.

Small, silvery mullet fish

leap in front of them.

Alligators snooze on the shore.

Long-legged herons wade in the mud.

Sam is old enough now to eat plants
like other manatees.
He finds a bed of water hyacinths.
Ummmmmmm!
They taste good.
Manatees graze on floating hyacinths
like cows in a pasture.
Sam pokes his whiskered face into the plants.
He tugs at them with the two sides
of his divided upper lip.
He pulls them into his mouth.
Munch! Munch! Munch!
His flat teeth crush and grind the hyacinths.

Sam needs lots of plants to feed
his growing body.
He eats many pounds of plants each day.
Sam gets rounder and bigger.

Sam rests when he is tired.
He floats near the surface
or lies on the river bottom.
But he can't stay down more than five minutes.
He must come up to breathe.
Sometimes Sam pops up near
fishing boats and surprises the fishermen.

CHAPTER

Sam leaves his mother when he is two years old.

He goes off on his own.

Like other manatees, he spends the next few years
swimming along the seacoast in the warm months
and returning to the rivers in the cooler season.

When Sam isn't eating,

he goes exploring.

He swims around wooden pilings.

He searches under old piers.

He squeezes his big body through narrow places.

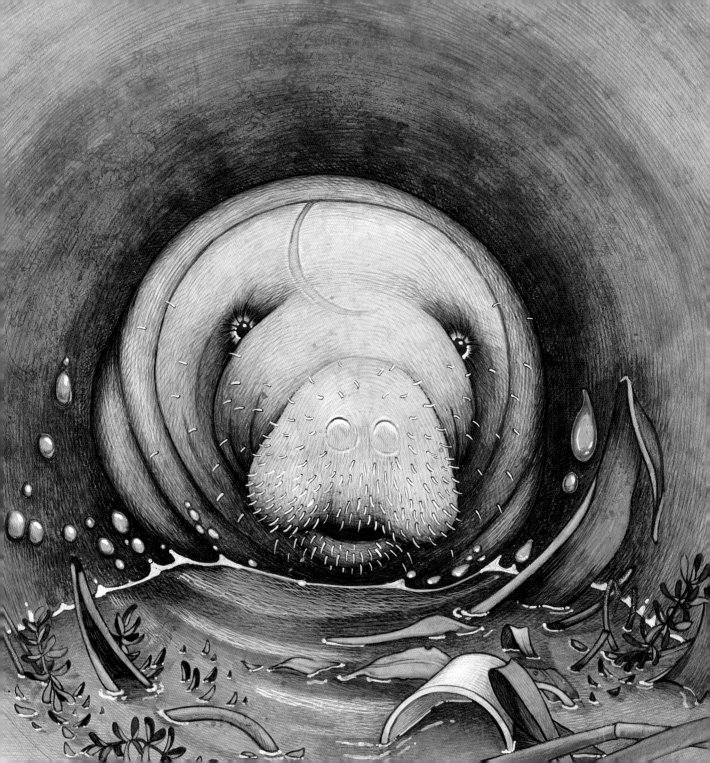

One day Sam swims off into a canal.

He finds a new place to explore.

It is a big, round cement pipe.

He flips his tail. He pushes with his flippers.

He wiggles and twists. He squirms half in.

But then he can't get out again.

Sam is stuck in a sewer drain.

People hear Sam's cries.

He is bruised, bleeding, and weak.

They try to help him, but Sam is too big.

Sam is nine feet long. He weighs as much as eight people.

Sam can't be moved from the drain.

So there he stays—half-in, half-out.

He gets hungry and grows weaker.

More people come.

Boys and girls run to see the stuck manatee.

Newspaper people come too.

But no one can budge poor Sam.

They call the Seaquarium.

Men come with trucks.

They pull Sam out of the sewer drain and
onto a stretcher.

A crane lifts the stretcher
and lowers Sam carefully onto a padded truck.

It will take Sam to the Seaquarium.

The newspaper people call him Sewer Sam.

"Good-bye, Sewer Sam!"
the boys and girls call.

Sam has a new home now.

He lives in a round, cement pool.

Keepers care for Sam.

They feed him lettuce leaves and bananas.

Soon Sam is feeling well again.

He swims around and around the pool.

But there is nothing for him to explore here.

Visitors come to the Seaquarium.
They come to see the killer whales
dance on their tails.
They come to see the dolphins
jump through hoops.
They come to see the sea lions
catch and balance balls.
Hardly anyone comes to see Sam.
Sam cannot do any tricks.

A year passes slowly. The keepers think Sam is lonely.

They put him in another pool so he can have company.

Two other manatees live there.

Sam follows them around and around.

But they are happy together, and they don't want Sam.

Poor Sam!

The keepers finally decide to return him to a river.

But they worry.

Will Sam remember how to live in a river

after so much time in the Seaquarium?

The keepers slip a stretcher under Sam.

They fold his flippers in so they won't get hurt.

Sam is lifted out of the pool and into a soft, padded box.

He is covered with moist cloths.

"Good luck, Sam. We'll miss you," a keeper calls.

Sam is lifted to a truck and taken to an airplane.

The pilot flies Sam to Crystal River,

six hundred miles away.

Many manatees spend the winter

in the warm waters there.

Sam has never flown before.

But he is calm and still, even when he is sprayed

with water to keep his skin wet.

Sam is lowered into the water.

Men in rubber suits help Sam out of the box.

They swim with him, but Sam tries to hide

from them in a clump of weeds.

What's this? Food?

Munch! Munch! Munch!

Sam eats the weeds.

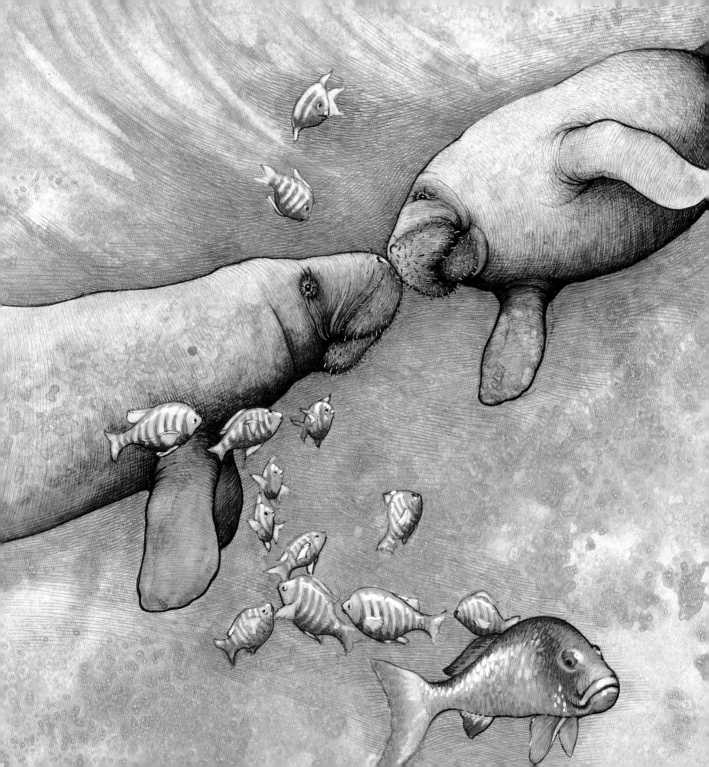

Days pass.

The men watch over Sam.

He seems happy to be free again.

Other manatees are swimming in the river.

Eep! Eep! Eep!

Sam calls them.

He flips his tail and swims to them.

One manatee turns to face Sam.

He puts his snout right up to Sam's.

They rub noses.

They rub whiskers.

The manatees begin to twist and roll.

They pop up and down.

They play follow-the-leader.

They swim off together.

Good-bye, Sam!

ABOUT SEA COWS

A sea cow is a large, gentle animal that lives in warm seas. There are two kinds of sea cows living today. One kind is called a dugong. It lives far away in the Indian Ocean. The other kind is the manatee. Manatees live nearer to us, in the warm parts of the Atlantic Ocean and in the Caribbean Sea.

Once there were many thousands of sea cows. Sailors saw them lifting their heads above the waves. The sea cows looked like beautiful ladies to some lonely sailors. It isn't easy to mistake the wrinkled sea cow for a pretty woman. But that is how stories of mermaids—half women, half fish—came to be told.

There are few sea cows left now. Some manatees still swim near the shores of Florida and in its warm bays,

rivers, and canals. These manatees, like Sam, belong to the species *Trichechus manatus.*

The manatees' ancestors lived on land ages ago. They grazed on plants and walked on four legs. Then some of these ancient animals went into the sea. The offspring of these creatures changed over thousands of years. Their forelegs became flippers. Their hind legs disappeared. Only toenails remain today to show that manatees once had feet. Manatees look nothing like their cousins, the elephants, who stayed on the land.

This story about Sam is based on events that led to Sam's care at the Seaquarium in Miami, Florida, and to his release thirteen months later in the Crystal River on Florida's west coast. The helpful, friendly manatees clear Florida waterways that are choked with weeds. They are now protected from harm by law.

For further information
on manatees, contact:

Save the Manatee Club
500 N. Maitland Ave.
Maitland, FL 32751
1-800-432-JOIN